Disney

Tangled

Level 3

Re-told by: Jocelyn Potter & Andy Hopkins
Series Editor: Rachel Wilson

T0345642

Pearson Education Limited
KAO Two
KAO Park, Harlow,
Essex, CM17 9NA, England
and Associated Companies throughout the world.

ISBN: 978-1-2923-4676-2

This edition first published by Pearson Education Ltd 2020

7 9 10 8 6

Copyright © 2020 Disney Enterprises, Inc. All rights reserved.

Set in Heinemann Roman Special, 14pt/23pt
Printed by Neografia, Slovakia

All rights reserved; no part of this publication may be reproduced, stored in a retrieval system, or transmitted in any form or by any means, electronic, mechanical, photocopying, recording, or otherwise, without the prior written permission of the Publishers.

Published by Pearson Education Limited

Acknowledgments
123RF.com: Vladimir Vinogradov 23
Alamy Stock Photo: Cavan 26, Jan Sochor 26
Shutterstock.com: Africa Studio 24, mary416 27, tomertu 22

For a complete list of the titles available in the Pearson English Readers series, visit www.pearsonenglishreaders.com.

Alternatively, write to your local Pearson Education office or
to Pearson English Readers Marketing Department,
Pearson Education, KAO Two, KAO Park, Harlow, Essex, CM17 9NA

In This Book

Rapunzel
A princess with golden hair

Mother Gothel
A very bad, old woman

The King and Queen
Rapunzel's parents; important people in their country

Flynn
A young man, a thief

Maximus
A horse with the castle guards

The Stabbington Brothers
Two big, strong thieves

Before You Read

Introduction

One day, a princess is born in a castle. Rapunzel has golden hair—*magic* hair. Mother Gothel wants that magic, and she takes the baby away. Can Rapunzel's parents find her again? Can *she* find *them*?

Activities

1 **Look at the picture. Choose the right answer.**

1 Mother Gothel is *inside / outside* the tower.
2 Mother Gothel is *brushing / climbing up* Rapunzel's hair.

2 **Look at the pictures on pages 1 to 3. Discuss these questions. What do you think?**

1 Why do Mother Gothel and Rapunzel live in a tower?
  a Because Rapunzel's parents live there.
  b Because Mother Gothel is hiding Rapunzel from the world.

2 Why is Rapunzel's hair important in the story?
  a Because it is golden hair.
  b Because it is magic hair.

"What's this?" the old woman thinks. "A magic flower!"
The beautiful golden flower can heal people. It can also make
them young.
Mother Gothel's face and body change. She's young again!
"This flower's mine!" she says, and hides it.

The King is very sad because his wife is sick.

His guards find the magic flower and bring it to him. It heals the Queen and a princess is born.

Now, the magic is in the baby's golden hair.

Mother Gothel wants the magic back and climbs into the
castle. She cuts some hair from the baby, but it turns brown!
"Oh, no! I have to take the child," she thinks.
She carries Rapunzel to a tall tower in the forest.

For years, they live in the tower.
Mother Gothel goes out, but Rapunzel never leaves the tower.
"You can't go outside. It's dangerous," Mother Gothel tells her.
Rapunzel's hair grows very long. She works and plays happily.
She's always busy.

Every year on Rapunzel's birthday, there are lanterns in the sky. The day before her eighteenth birthday, Rapunzel says, "I want to see the lights tomorrow!"

"What? No, Rapunzel," Mother Gothel says. "Don't ask to leave this tower again." Then she goes out.

Flynn is a thief with a crown in his bag. He's running
from the castle guards and their horse, Maximus.
Where can he hide? He climbs up the tower.

BANG! Rapunzel hits him.
Then she finds the crown. She ties
Flynn to a chair.
"You can have the crown tomorrow,"
Rapunzel says. "But first, take me
to the lights."
"You mean the *lanterns*? Okay,"
he answers.
They leave the tower. Flynn goes first.
Then Rapunzel throws her golden hair
from the window and climbs down.

In the tower, Mother Gothel finds the crown and a poster.
But where's Rapunzel? Is she with Flynn Rider?
Outside, Rapunzel's excited. But the guards, Maximus, and two
more thieves—the Stabbington Brothers—are looking for Flynn.

Mother Gothel finds the Stabbingtons.

"You can have this crown," she says, "but you can get *more*
money for *Rapunzel*. The King and Queen are looking for her.
She's their daughter."

"Forget the crown. Let's find her!" the thieves laugh.

Rapunzel and Flynn run through the forest and jump into
the river. They swim underwater and escape from the guards
and the Stabbingtons.

They stop for the night because they're tired.

"*Ow!* My hand hurts!" Flynn says.

"Give me your hand," Rapunzel says.

She puts her golden hair around it.

"It feels better!" Flynn is very surprised. "How did you *do* that?"

Rapunzel laughs. "My hair's magic. It can heal people.

But I can never cut it."

Mother Gothel finds Rapunzel.

"I'm *not* coming home," Rapunzel says. "I have a new friend."

"Ha!" Mother Gothel laughs. "He only wants *this*!" She holds up the crown.

"No, he doesn't!" Rapunzel says, but she hides the crown from Flynn.

The next morning, they arrive at the city.
People are dancing in the streets!
"It's my birthday and this evening I can see the lanterns!"
Rapunzel thinks. She sees a picture of the King, the Queen,
and the princess with golden hair.

In the evening, Rapunzel and Flynn watch the beautiful lanterns from a boat. Rapunzel gives Flynn the crown.
"I don't want it—I want *you*," Flynn thinks.
He leaves Rapunzel in the boat and takes the crown to the Stabbingtons. But the Stabbingtons want Rapunzel.
They tie Flynn to a boat and send it away.

Rapunzel watches the boat.
"Flynn's leaving me!" she thinks,
and she escapes into the forest.
Mother Gothel hits the Stabbingtons
and Rapunzel comes back.
"You were right, Mother" she cries.

The guards catch Flynn, and then they catch
the Stabbingtons.

Flynn sees them and he's very angry. "How did you know
about Rapunzel?!"

"It was Mother Gothel," the Stabbingtons tell him.

Flynn escapes and rides quickly to the tower.

Back at the tower, Rapunzel remembers the picture of the princess. Suddenly, she understands …

"That's *me*! *I'm* the princess!" she shouts at Mother Gothel. "You only want me for my magic hair! You *need* me!"

"Rapunzel!" Flynn calls.

Rapunzel's hair comes down from the window and he climbs up.

But Rapunzel is tied up!

Mother Gothel angrily cuts him with some glass.

"No!" Rapunzel cries—but Flynn is dying. "Please, can I heal him?" Rapunzel asks Mother Gothel. "Then you can take me away."

"Okay," Mother Gothel answers.

She runs to Flynn.

"Don't do it," he says weakly, and then cuts Rapunzel's hair. The hair turns brown! The magic goes and Mother Gothel dies. Rapunzel holds Flynn. "Don't go," she cries. A golden tear falls on his face and heals him.

At the castle, Rapunzel runs into the arms of her parents, the King and Queen. Having and holding their daughter again is their dream. They all cry happy tears.

Rapunzel smiles at them and takes Flynn's hand. This is *her* dream.

After You Read

1 **Match the sentences and the pictures.**

1 The magic flower makes her younger.
2 The magic flower heals her.
3 Rapunzel's magic hair heals him.

 A

 B

 C

2 **Answer the questions.**

1 Where is Rapunzel born?
2 Where does she live for eighteen years?
3 Where does she see a picture of her parents?

3 **Finish the sentences. Discuss answers with a friend.**

1 Mother Gothel takes Rapunzel from her parents because …
2 The guards want to catch Flynn because …
3 Rapunzel's hair turns brown because …

Picture Dictionary

city

crown

cut

forest

golden

guard

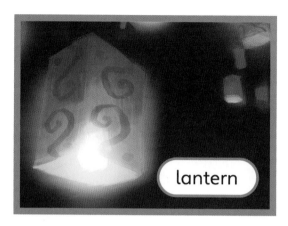

lantern

sky

street

tear

tie

tower

Phonics

Say the sounds. Read the words.

ng

long

king

nk

drink

think

Say the rhyme.

Rapunzel is home. It's the first day of spring.
We're having a party, in front of the King.

Let's have a dance, enjoy food and drink.
Is Rapunzel excited? What do you think?

Values

Stay busy.

For eighteen years, Rapunzel can't go outside. She gets bored, but she tries to use her time well.

I can make things.

I can paint the walls of the tower. Hmm, looks good!

I can dance and clean the floor at the same time!

But one day, I'd like to see the world …

Find Out

Why do people use lanterns?

In the old days, people used lanterns at night. Lanterns were in their houses and in the streets. These days, people don't have to use lanterns because they have electricity. Today, people like lanterns because they make a beautiful light.

making a paper lantern

In many countries around the world, people make paper lanterns and use them in their festivals.

In Hawaii, people put lanterns on the ocean. They remember the brave people of their country.

In China, there's a colorful lantern festival in spring. Some lanterns are animal shapes.

brave a *brave* person is not afraid of things